A Foreign Home

Áine Griffin

Copyright © 2022 Áine Griffin

Ibbetson Street Press
25 School Street
Somerville MA 02143

www.ibbetsonpress.com

Ibbetson Street Press
Endicott College Young Writer Series

ISBN: 978-1-6781-9206-8

edited by
Emily (Pineau) Lacey (Endicott College)
Book design by S.R. Glines (iscspress.com)
fonts: 1942 Report,Alegreya, & Brandon Grotesque

Acknowledgments

Thank you to Emily Lacey for editing this chapbook; I appreciate your encouragement, enthusiasm, and insight more than you know. I also want to thank Doug Holder and Dan Sklar for this opportunity. Thank you also to my wonderful friends and family for being my constant support. Finally, every word was written in loving memory of my Mum and fellow writer, Joanne Fiske—I felt your joy while I was working on this project the most.

Introduction

"A Foreign Home" is a confessional collection of poems and short stories interwoven with the themes of lust, body image, femininity, loss, and healing. The collection explores how when we feel lost and lonely, we look backwards for a home instead of inwards, and to others' hearts and bodies for acceptance instead of our own. Moving from more lighthearted pieces about the young desire to feel wanted and seen, to more weighted pieces about coping with loss and recognizing one's reflection in the mirror, "A Foreign Home" portrays the raw journey of finding peace with all facets of one's self.

The title concept of the "foreign" home has a few central meanings which are explored throughout the book. First, is the idea of the body being a "foreign home" to our souls, exploring how our sense of self is deeply tied to our physical bodies, yet we can often feel extremely detached from them. Second, is the way in which our "home" is often defined by the people we love, and how after a significant loss, the world around us can feel foreign, unstable, and difficult to navigate. Finally, is the literal concept of a "foreign" home as the result of immigration, and the ways we define ourselves culturally through homes that no longer exist, or which we no longer inhabit.

In terms of the writing process, I tried to rid myself of the image of the audience I was writing for, which has often controlled what I chose to write in the past, and instead focused on writing honestly. Though largely fiction, I framed the pieces around moments I felt held the most unfiltered truth; lines from old journal entries, conversations with close friends, and any words or sentiments that came from a place of vulnerability. In facing the parts of myself that have always been easier to hide from, I hope I can encourage others to do the same. When we understand and love ourselves for all that we are, we can start to make our homes feel a bit less foreign.

Contents

A Foreign Home

For South Boston

When I think of the city I knew as a child
I think of my grandmother's back deck,
tucked in between the triple-deckers.
It was just a few potted plants,
a chemtrailed square of sky,
and a slice of hot city air,
but it gave me hard ground
beneath my feet
and breath
pounding through my bones.

For ten years I sat out there,
a sticky cherry slush smile
permanently smeared across my face,
counting down the glory days
while planes whirred overhead
and church bells sang in the distance.

My Mamo and her lovely satin voice
telling me stories of the homeland,
Johnny next door, with his midday cigarettes
and his wife-beaters,
jump ropes and scraped knees,
front stoops and the daily Herald,
boys with backwards caps and mean streaks.
That's all I knew of the city,
that's all I knew of the world.

✣

When I turned thirteen
my grandmother's porch chair
lay empty,
a vacant throne amid the potted plants.
All spring, I sat out there with the geraniums and Johnny
and together we grieved
as her breath,
her ration of cement and air,
was released back to the city.

In my naivety I could only mourn
the loss at the tip of my nose.
I couldn't see
my Mamo's vacant deck
was just one of hundreds,
a single drop in the wave of change
washing over the city.

‡

Last year Johnny's building was sold
for close to a million.

He had one last cigarette
standing in his back door.
The ashes embered in the old white dish
as he blew a final stream of smoke
into the July air.
I watched it dance up to the clouds,
spiral in the gap between the buildings,
and disappear.

It was a quiet tribute,
a lonely goodbye.

I wonder if the man who bought the apartment
a young thirty-something from Rhode Island
who surfed and worked downtown,
I wonder if he ever thought about the man who left
the ashtray on his porch.
I wonder if before investing in an urban property
if he thought about whose backs he stood on,
who owned that little square of cement and sky and air before
him—

Because I don't always think about it
when people ask me where I'm from.

I don't always think about
the hundreds of back decks
pressed between the apartments
and the generations that called them home.

And how one day,
when the final front stoop,
when the final slice of sky
is sold
the air of the neighborhood
will belong to new lungs,

and the city I knew as a child
for all its beauty
and all its ugly

will breathe no more.

Edwardian Summer

I spent the summer in subtle bliss.
Strolling from one part-time shift to the next,
dancing with my toes in the sand of impermanence,
knee-deep in the refreshing waves of inconsequentiality.

Nights spent meeting childhood friends,
legs crossed on the old seaport dock,
laughing from our stomachs in the hot city air.

Coming alive with a curly-headed stranger in his backseat,
no talk of who we were or where we were going,
just a backwards Red Sox cap and a very-best bra.

And everyone has always told me
I should want more than this.
Told me that no satisfaction comes from letting the air simply
flow through me,
that one day I'd have to grow up and learn to cultivate every
ounce of breath.

And maybe it's true.

But this morning, when I got an email
about my tuition being overdue,
my throat clenched as I realized
I am just two years away
from being handed a $100,000 deed
to a life I committed to when I was seventeen,
to a life I'm not even sure I want.

And as dawn goes down today,
and I pack up my last teenage summer in the city,

I can't help but feel
like a tantruming toddler being told to leave the pool,
screaming and flailing in my neon plastic floaties,
begging for just five more minutes
to splash around.

Love Poem

I felt hopeless last night
scrolling through the beautiful cookie-cutter girls
you held in the daylight.
Not just because I was jealous but

because if that's all it'd take
I know I would do it.
I would dye my hair back blonde
and lose the weight around my stomach.

I'd perfect the way they exist,
how they speak, and what they joke about,
the way they never get excited.

I'd keep things on the surface,
tell you how hot that was after sex,
not wring my body out the window
and ask if you felt as free as me.

I'd never paint anything but pretty landscapes
and be the chillest motherfucker
and the brand of wild
people love.

I would shove myself back into all of those boxes
and lay my tiny shrunken frame down at your feet
and forever play the part of the person
you always saw yourself with,

one word
and I'd do it.

First World February

I have found in the dark depths of winter, when the days are short and the months are hopelessly long, there comes a certain ache in the pit of my soul that I never learned how to cure. It isn't some great pang of pain, or an open bleeding wound, just a slow and steady weight pulling me from my core. Most of the time I don't realize it's there at all.

It was a cold night mid-February. Some friends of mine were going out; we weren't particularly close, but we grew up in the same grid of concrete, and that proved a strong enough commonality for us to call each other friends. Unbreakably unbothered, they paid no heed to tears, or scraped knees, or people like me, but they knew how to dance until the early morning, knew how to arch their backs and lose their minds until even St. Peter turned his head. I couldn't even tell you if I liked them—I couldn't tell you if they liked themselves. We just kept each other around for nights like these, drinking and dancing our way through the depths of February.

I got ready slowly. There was such fun in showering, scrubbing myself to the bone and then watching all the grime, all the evidence of daily life, spiral in coconut-scented suds down the drain. When I finished, my raw skin glowed pink in the steamy bathroom mirror. The pale slope of my stomach, the angry red bumps by my vagina, the white of my toes gripping the tile; I waited an extra moment before grabbing a towel, just to marvel at the ugliness of it all.

Across from me, my phone buzzed from on top of the toilet. I paddled over and picked it up. The foggy screen lit up with notifications: a text from my aunt, a few snapchats, a group chat

I never participated in. A pile of emails, a pile of assignments, a pile of people to let down. Too much. I ignored it all and scrolled through Instagram, mindlessly watching the lives of loose acquaintances float by my eyes. Little people in little boxes, living little lives on a little screen, liked by little me.

Big me.

Old me.

Five-foot-nine me.

Cold. Damp. I kept getting ready. I flung on a layer of instant tan, fried my hair into an acceptable shape, and filled in a more life-filled face over my own. It made me nostalgic for dressing up my dolls when I was young, tirelessly preparing them for their all-important make-believe lives.

When I was dressed, I went back to the bathroom mirror. I looked at my neck, my breasts, the freckle on the side of my underarm, the bit of concealer that had crusted over on my forehead. I knew they were all mine, and I theirs, but the idea that it was the same entity thinking my thoughts and moving my body frightened me to an inexplicable degree, and the longer I looked at my reflection the more difficult it became to breathe.

A buzz. My phone. A shallow breath. The Uber was outside. I forced myself to pry my knuckles off the porcelain sink. I wanted so badly to stay in that pale pink bathroom, staring at my reflection until my breath ran out. But my beautifully mean friends were waiting, and I'd hate to disappoint them.

II.

The three of us went downtown. The car dropped us off on a corner a block away from the bar. I looked at them skipping and laughing ahead of me. And then, for a moment, I was above us, watching our little bodies dancing down the concrete. Myself and my fairy friends in their lace and leather—how beautiful they were, I thought, how ethereal. (Bitches, every last one of us.)

I told myself I'd only have a few drinks, the way my mother used to say she'd only have a taste of dessert, or only pop into the shop for a look. I ended up spending everything I'd made that week, just for the thrill of letting it go. Like the dirty coconut suds in the shower, I watched the grime of the everyday, the paper proof of my existence, spiral away.

Rounds. Laughs. Pleasantries. Dancing. A bit of life in the dead of days, a prescribed spark in the dark depths of February. The bass of the music rattled through my bones until I couldn't distinguish between the beat shaking the room and the beat of blood in my head. I looked down at my wiry hands clinging to the edge of the table. I couldn't feel them and that brought me some sort of satisfaction.

"Is that really what you want though?" A man next to me asked. Wet eyes. Scruff.

"Hmm?"

"I mean is that really what you want to do with your degree?" I wondered what I had told him.

"I don't think I really know, yet, what I want."

"No?"

"Well I think, I think, I think that's my problem. Sometimes I feel like I don't actually want anything at all. Like, I think I'm one of those people who just keeps putting one foot in front of the other, one in front of the other, until... " I had wanted to say 'until they died,' but I could hear the immature melodramatics of it before it could leave my mouth.

"So what are you majoring in?" I asked instead. I reached for his arm. I knew, at least, I wanted it desperately, whatever he could give me. Drinks. Attention. Someone to stand beside as strangers a little longer.

"I think your friends are looking for you," he said, ignoring my question, ignoring my offer. I didn't see them. He disappeared. He thought I was an idiot. I could take most things but being thought of as an idiot wasn't one of them. I gripped the table harder.

A bathroom mirror. A version of myself staring back at me, smudgy, sly. I had forgotten what I looked like. The room was spinning in big glorious circles, I couldn't keep my eyes focused on the faces in front of me. The friends from earlier, the cool, unbreakable, fairy-like ones, they were glowing, laughing. How dare people call them bitches. Someone told me to stay away from the man I had spoken to at the bar, he wasn't worth my time. My own posse of sylphs, how magical. I clung to the stall door.

Back out amid the voices and the lights. Smoke in my lungs. Hot, stale, beautiful. I thought about how different this would all be in the summer. How sweet fresh warm air would taste, how much more manageable it all would seem when it was light out longer than it was dark. Across the sea of faces I saw a pair of eyes. The man from earlier. The scruff, the beady wet eyes, he was walking toward me.

It was nice to sway to the music. It was nice to rely on another body to hold up mine. His hands were on my back, on my ass, the familiar rush of dead adrenaline pulsed in my veins. I lifted my numb fingers and ran them through his hair. His deep blue eyes, I was swimming in them, sinking. I wrapped my arms around his neck to keep from going under. As I closed my eyes, his warm boozy breath met mine.

III.

The fairy friends and I went stumbling into the street. The cool ocean breeze blew in from the coast, and washed over my body. Soberness struck me. The air was cold, and there was the pit again, dizzy, heavy, and lonely, weighing down in my stomach.

I had the sudden urge to go rowing then. To go get grandad's old currach and go out by myself. Feel the dark waves push me and my little canvas ship up and down. When the night got choppy, the salt water would splash up against my face and soak my stupid party dress. And then alone in my little boat I could weep for you. I could tell you I was sorry and I was lost and for heaven's sake I didn't think I had it in me to row back to shore.

And I could say come with me, please, just come back with me. And you'd float down from the stars in your beautiful white dress and I'd steer us back to shore. We'd drink big cups of tea in the kitchen like the old days. I'd show you a Facebook photo of the guy from the bar and you'd poke fun at his mustache, and tell me he's handsome enough but not the boy for me, and I'd believe you. And you'll tell me I take things too seriously, too much to heart. That these years were meant for drinking and dancing and the thrill of kissing strangers in bars. And the night would be quiet because it's only the two of us awake and we'll catch up on years of memories, giggling away in the lamp light while Dad snores upstairs. And everything will be light and simple and perfect, and loneliness will be a feeling I only hear about in songs.

But you're not here and we can't stay up late drinking tea and talking. And holidays don't feel like holidays anymore. And birthdays don't feel like birthdays, and home hasn't felt like home in so, so long—

And now my friends, laughing like the sea, start taking the piss at how long I'd been staring in the distance. And they see the tears brim in my eyes and asked why the fuck I was crying, was it because that guy grabbed my ass at the bar? And I can't look at them and tell them I'm floating, just waiting till my arms give out and my ship gets swallowed by the waves. That each day I am trying to crawl my way back to shore.

IV.

I awoke in a sweaty bundle of flesh and bones, crumpled by the toilet. I looked up at the pale pink walls of the bathroom, their familiar faces smirking down at me. Birds chirped outside, and sunlight crept in the window. Everything looked so different in the air of the morning. So much lighter and simpler and easier. How on earth was I so dramatic just a few hours ago, I wondered, how did my body seem so heavy that I was ready to let all this beauty go, just to be free of its weight?

Then, like whiplash, the buzz of my phone lurking by my side made it all come crashing down once again. The pile of unanswered texts and messages bared their teeth at me from behind the cracked mask of the screen, and the familiar clench of anxiety hit my stomach.

Steadily, I pulled myself up off the tile, and heaved myself over to the sink. The same stupid face from the night before looked back at me. I watched her brush her teeth, rubbing the little brush up and down, up and down, until she frothed at the mouth. I watched her gargle mouthwash, and spit the sharp neon liquid back into the sink. I watched her rub the remnants of her makeup onto a hot face cloth, and tie her hair into a knot on top of her skull.

I still didn't know her. But I carried her like a doll from room to room, place to place. I poured hot coffee down her throat and washed her sordid skin and brought her on and off the city bus to work. I spent my money on making her comfortable, I paid her rent and bought her pleasant-smelling candles and told her she was a very good and very beautiful pile of bones even if I didn't believe it.

And one might say that's not progress or happiness or hope, but I was no longer putting one foot in front of the other until I died. I was putting one foot in front of the other until I felt alive again.

Twenty

I love pre-drinks that lead to hours of talking,
faces crinkled over plastic cups,
pouring out bottomless soul and
never making it to the party.

I love stolen glances, little shared smirks,
with the person you know you'll never sleep with;
late-night thoughts of them too treasured
to taint with anything tangible.

I love accidental meetings in the kitchen,
roommates dressed in wet hair and slippers,
nothing in common but the space to fill
while the water boils.

I love the faces so consistent
they become part of the landscape,
ever-reliable, like the blurry houses out the train window,
a constant, when nothing else seems to be.

I once wore rose-tinted glasses,
so the world wouldn't be so harsh on my eyes.
I lost them on a night-out last February,
and fell back in love with my life.

A Foreign Home

The waves almost swallowed me today,
almost kept me forever
in the cold September water of the bay.
My body went numb looking out at the horizon
as I became the space where the two blues met.

When they spit me back out,
I went home to my old friend hanging on the wall
and wondered why I recognized my reflection more
in the trees and in the sea,
in the stars and in the skyline,
than framed in this square of glass,
just a hard punch away from shattering.

I seem to know everyone in my life so well.
The sound of their footfalls on the stairs,
the smell of their pheromones and sweat and dirty laundry,
the way they tap their lips before they speak
and the saunter of their hips
and the little idiosyncrasies that come out when they're agitated.
But sometimes I can't quite believe
my body goes about the world
the same way theirs do.

I do not pray that one day I align my physicality and my psyche,
I pray I find peace in knowing I never will.

For I think when I stop looking for answers in breakable reflec-
tions
I'll be able to walk fearlessly between heaven and earth,
content with balancing on the horizon line,

knowing I am but the pulse of the universe incarnate,
and the body will always be a foreign home.

Freeing Lizzie

Lizzie was my best friend growing up. I loved her baby face and her lazy eye and her trusting nature. Loved her obsession with lizards and Barbies and giving inanimate objects names and personalities. Loved her dress-up box, her older brother, and her crinkled-nose laugh. Every inch of her was so unapologetic and perfect.

We experienced everything together, spending late nights cuddled under her comforter, sharing laughs and tears and secrets. It was as if I felt everything Lizzie felt—every burst of pride with the A's on her report card, every butterfly over her crushes, every sting of her schoolyard-scraped knees, every wishful dream, every pang of joy and sadness—we shared every morsel of it all.

The year we turned eleven, Lizzie started slipping through my fingers. I couldn't pinpoint a day or moment when we started to drift, but I know when we passed each other in the halls, I could see it in her eyes. She was letting go of me. There was no argument, no final goodbye, we just motionlessly watched the space between us grow wider and wider.

By twelve or thirteen we completely lost touch. Her family moved up the coast somewhere, she left without saying a word. After that I only knew her from the frames on my dresser.

At the end of eighth grade, the first letter came. It was scribbled on the back of a beat-up postcard from San Francisco. There was no signature, but it was written in that same voice that whispered in my ear for all those years.

I need a friend, it said. I want to be seen. I just want someone to
hear me.

Once she wrote that first admittance, she couldn't stop. For
years the letters poured in. Some on napkins, some on torn
notebook paper, some on the back of old homework pages. Little
confessionals about her life, excerpts about different events and
people, how she was feeling. And from these letters, written in
the early hours of the mornings we once spent together, I could
feel her world again through the foggy space between us.

The connection was subtle—I didn't know her emotions in as
much color and vibrancy as when we were children. They hit me
like a far cry from the distance that I could just about hear if I
listened close enough.

9/12/10

It scares me a bit, sometimes, how many years ahead of me I
have. Sometimes the days and weeks feel really long, and they all
feel the same. And I'm really bad at school. I can't seem to care
about it any longer. But life is okay. I can't complain. I just feel a
bit trapped by everything, that's all.

11/4/10

I met some girls who seemed nice. I hope they liked me. I think I
was really awkward.

5/16/11

I failed two classes this year. I don't know how it happened. I'm
so ashamed I could throw up. It's difficult to feel things lately,
and everyone's yelling at me to focus. To move on. I wish so bad-

ly I could listen. I sit at my desk for hours trying to get anything done. I shoved my hand in a closing car door yesterday. It wasn't as painful as I thought it would be.

8/25/11

I hope no one ever reads these, they are brutally dramatic. Everything's fine. Today was my birthday, I felt really loved.

2/15/12

I think a lot about you. I worry you would be disappointed in me. I don't know why I can't seem to do better than this.

3/11/15

I have a boyfriend named Thomas, he's wonderful, the type of boy we always dreamt about. He's handsome and kind and he has brought me so much happiness. But I am leaning on him and I think he knows it. It's too much pressure for an eighteen-year-old to be someone else's joy. I wish I wasn't so fearful of life without him.

12/10/15

I wish I was smaller.

1/1/16

I left Thomas before he could leave me. I don't think I really loved him anyways, I just loved feeling like the type of person who could be in a relationship. Loved feeling that pretty and wanted.

6/17/17

I blinked and another year went by, I don't know how it is summer again. I don't think it is me moving my feet through all these months. The only time I know what I want or what I'm feeling is when I write it down.

8/18/18

I'm trying not to squeeze myself into boxes anymore. Perhaps then I will feel more alive. I bought a dog and moved up north, away from Mum and everyone.

Then, for a while, the bits of late-night writing stopped. Until, perfectly formatted on a piece of pretty stationery, I was sent a letter not quite like the rest.

Life has been really wonderful lately. I've been seeing a therapist, her name is Stacey.

Anyways, I'm really writing to say I am so sorry you didn't even get a warning or an explanation, when I left you all those years ago. Everything had changed so quickly. It's like all of a sudden I was experiencing a new type of hurt, one so much more brutal than scraped knees or anything you and I had ever dealt with before. It was all so heavy and confusing, and I suppose I thought if I let all that new pain touch you, if I let you really feel everything for what it was, you wouldn't survive.

It was instinct I think, to walk away.

But even though I didn't have a choice I want you to know I still regret it. Because without you, I have been a shell of my true self. I have gone through the motions for ten years, never really feeling present in anything, never wholly showing up for anyone, never growing. I was so afraid of feeling anything negative, I slowly chose to feel nothing at all. I still don't quite know what I am doing but I'm trying to come back to myself.

I don't think I'll be writing to you again for some time. But know I think of you now more than ever.

With Love,
Lizzie

I tucked the letter away into my heart. I had a feeling she was right, it would be the last letter I was receiving.

I bathed in the silence for months, until last July, when I was floating through a grocery store in Northern Oregon. I was aimlessly watching the people pass by my eyes—when there she was— just a few feet ahead of me. A woman in a long skirt covered in little vintage flowers, leaning over the heads of lettuce. She had changed; had small lines by her eyes and across her forehead, a tattoo across her shoulder, and an extra foot of height.

But it was Lizzie.

The fogginess of the store cleared from around her, and for the first time in a decade I saw the world in sharp, glorious colors.

Every inch of who she was, every scar and smile line, was standing there before me.

I am so beautiful, I thought. And I have made it so far.

Loch Phreacháin

Bhí sé ánn mar bhí fado mé feín agus e feín ag faíl reitigh
ag tabhairt aghaidh ar na sleibhte uaigneach agus ar Loch
Phreacháin.

Ach dhúisigh mise i nua Eabhrach i bhfad ó loch phreacháin.
Bhi mo bhrionglóid chomh láidir nach imigh sí as mo cheann go
rinneadh mé suas mintinn go dtabharainn cuart amháin eile ar
Loch Phreacháin.

Is iomaí loch a thriáil mé féin agus mo chara ón teach dóite go
barr Uachtarard ach bualadh Loch Phreacháin leí breac rua ní
raibh sé le fáil.

Tá mé eirigh as an obair agus níl tada am ach ám. Fuair mo
thicéad leí cuairt amháin eile thabhairt ar Loch Phreacháin.

Bhí na crainnte ulig fásta anois agus ba deacair á shiúil ach ní
raibh tada leí mé stopadh go bhfeicinn Loch Phreacháin.

Chaith mé cupla uair ag iascach ag cuartú breac rua nach raibh
ánn ní raibh sè ar nós fado ní dheachaigh muid ariamh follamh
ó Loch Phreacháin.

Is iomaí rud chuaigh tríd mintinn agus mé cuimhniú arfadó
nuar a bhíodh mé féin agus mo chara anseo ag iascach agus ag
comhrá.

Chuir mé paidir le nanam agus d'fhag mé slan Loch Phreacháin
a ní dhéanamh mé dearmad ar chomhairle mo chara.

Anois tá mé ar ais i nua Eachrach agus cheapadh nach bhfeadach uaigneas bheith ort ánn ach tá mo chroí sa briste agus mé ag cuimhniú ar Loch Phreacháin.

Rinneadh mé uachta an lá cheanna chuir píosa ina lcr dúirt mé la mo chlann nuair a thiocfadhas mo lá sa gan mé fhagál i bhfad ós cionn cláir ach mé chreamatáil sciopaí agus mo luatha scaipeadh ar bhruacha Loch Phreacháin.

Generations of Strong Women

The fabric stretched thin across my back,
bunched in my underarms so tight it pinched,
I stand, cursing my broad shoulders
sweating in the fluorescent lights of Marshall's.

Broad shoulders like my Granny's,
a wide tall frame, sturdy ribs and strong hands
bred into the bloodline from generations of
carrying pounds of turf and flour and little ones.

But there isn't any turf to carry anymore.
No coarse, wild mountains to climb,
just a leather tote bag with a few books
that I drag on and off the green line
to work and school.

And as I stand looking foolish
in a sweater too small
I wonder how we got from there to here.

How she worried about where the next meal would come from,
and I worry about how many calories it will have.
How I can't seem to wear it proudly,
the body she gave me,
the body of the unbreakable matriarch.
How I always slouch a few inches off my height,
collapse my shoulders in,
fold myself smaller,
take up less space,

to be more feminine, perhaps,
easier to love.

Meaningless Sex

It's Meaningless
that we picked each other from the internet
like ordering a box of takeout, or a new shirt.
Not necessarily each other's first choice,
just the closest version of what we wanted
with the lowest shipping price.

Meaningless
that we didn't know each other's phone numbers, or last names,
but we held each other,
skin to skin, heartbeat to heartbeat,
laying in bedrooms we knew
we'd never get to memorize.

Meaningless
that a stranger could leave me breathless,
wildly alive and wildly worthless,
forever dancing between the costumes of
self-empowerment and self-destruction.

Meaningless
that we were the image of the heartless generation—
just two turn-of-the-century babies,
raised on Disney princesses and internet porn,
Sunday school and Albert Camus,

hooking up in the back of a parking lot
on the broken logic
that nothing means anything
until we want it to.

Hail Holy Queen

I watch the men go about the world so unafraid to take up every morsel of space
and I can't help but think
it must all be because
from the moment I was old enough to listen in Mass
I was told God is a He and God had a Son,
and God is almighty and God will come again,
and until then God should be given as much room as possible,
in the homes and hearts of the poor sinners,
until then God deserves every inch and breath of a woman's grace
to make money and be brave and receive all the blind praise and faith
as his predecessor.

Because I never heard a "she" in the holy trinity,
whispering my Hail Mary's,
and tangling myself in the paradoxical expectation
of the Virgin Mother—
it's no wonder I never felt quite enough,
chasing a goal
so unattainable.

And perhaps one would say
we've moved past that paradox of the Virgin Mother in the literal sense
but I can't help but feel we're all still held by the twisted story of misunderstood Mary.
Because the woman can live without the restraints of marriage, motherhood, and celibacy,
she can sleep with who she pleases
and no one will despise her for choosing not to have children.

But somehow the hope is that she still giggles at a man's touch.
The expectation is that she still carries herself
with an air of having something she has yet to experience,
that she looks young with smooth, hairless skin and
narrow hips and a petite girlish frame—

But, with her girlish virgin looks,
she also has the air of wisdom of a mother.
A gentleness and patience and sense of responsibility—
that she keeps herself and her world together,
and knows just how to care for a child,
no matter if they are three or thirty.

And sometimes I get so confused between wanting to let go
of my female body
and wanting to be free
of the internalized ideal of Mary.

I dress in big, baggy clothes
where you can't tell what sorts of bits are hiding underneath.
And I am so grateful I live in a time and place
where no one feels the need to rip them off me
and decide who my body says I am.

But I have come to understand that this alone does not bring me
satisfaction.

I want to let the rolls of my stomach hang free.
I want to walk with my broad shoulders stretched open and
wide to the sky.
I want to let the muscles on my arms be admired and the slope
of my breast lusted after

and the touch of my thighs be a sacred and praised place.
I want to be proud of every inch of the she/her, and exist not as
the opposite of man but as their counterpart: a sexual, fruitful,
divine feminine being.

No blueprint, No Madonna nor Magdalene,
nothing attached to my body but my soul.

I am Not What I am

My beautiful Juliet, he tells her,
you have won my heart.
My Ophelia, my Desdemona, my Rosalind,
you know me better than any soul,
and I am devoted to every piece of you,
so perfectly designed for me.

The poor fucker can't see she's Iago.

A master of performance, of blurring the line between phenom-
enon and essence—
she doesn't love you, fool,
the girl who professes to wear her heart on her sleeve.

After years of being who everyone needed,
she just loves knowing
she is a good enough actress
to never be alone.

Knife to the Hide

My father used to tell me all sorts of stories when I was younger. He was really great at it. Anecdotes from growing up, old faerie stories, that sort of thing. I spent my childhood nights fighting sleep to hear them through to the end.

I hadn't thought about those stories in a long time, but for whatever reason one of them has been crossing my mind lately. He grew up in Ireland, you know that. The village where he was raised is far in the countryside in an area called Connemara. It's an unusual area, really, not like the postcards you see of Ireland with their miles of rich greenery. By his home, there is an inlet of sea on one side, salt air and seafoam and swans. On the other, there is all this rocky land. Fields interrupted by mountains, bogland, ponies, stones, sheds. The first time he took my mother back there I was two. She wrote on a postcard home to Boston that his house was "way out there." She also wrote that she was so happy. I think about that postcard sometimes.

I'm sure I've told you about all the summers I spent in Connemara growing up, but I never got to take you there and it's one of those places you have to see for yourself to understand. The eeriness of the sea in between the mountains. The roughness of the land. The improbability that anything could grow there, that people could survive off of such rocky earth. "To hell or to Connacht", as history goes.

Anyways, the story. When my father was about six or seven the family cow died. It was a shock, for she wasn't very old, and it was expected they'd have her another good few years, and that she would breed a good few more calves. From what my father told me they only had the one cow, and they didn't have a lot of money, so it was really a blow to the household for her to die before her time. He also had an attachment to her, of course. I suppose you grow to really love any animal if you see them every day.

Well, from what my father told me, my grandad was a tough man and a stubborn man, and he wasn't going to bury the cow without knowing why it died. He was convinced she had eaten something toxic that had been carelessly discarded in her field by the roadside.

The night she died, he dragged my young father out in the dead of night, to the shed behind the house where the body lay. He handed him a flashlight to hold, then pulled his knife from his pocket, and crouched down to the dead thing.

He took the knife to her hide, tearing the carcass straight down the middle, ripping the animal open. My father watched in horror—the grey and red sludge poured out of its open frame, as my grandad went scavenging through the bones and blood and organs for his answer. He thought he was going to faint, watching the lovely cow he had fed and milked each day for years be torn to bits, but he cared far too much of what his father thought of him to so much as flinch.

At last my grandad rose triumphantly. In his hand was a broken piece of battery that had been lodged in the cow's intestines.

"Now," he said. "What did I tell you?"

He wiped the knife off in satisfaction, and put the shard of poison in his pocket.

"We'll bury her tomorrow. Buachaill maith. Good boy."

My father always tells that story in admiration of his father, proud and amazed by his intuition and wisdom when it came to the animals. Sometimes I wondered if he really told it because the image of the young cow being ripped in half never really left him.

Anyways, that story has been on my mind the past few days, and then I had a dream the other night. I was at my grandparents' house, wandering the same fields my father grew up in. It was cold and the rain was lashing, but I felt tranquil in the midst of it all, just happy to be back in Connemara. The place always reminded me of the carefreeness of youth, and I felt nostalgically free to be back there.

Eventually I came to the shed, the one where the cow had died in all those years ago. Walking the path up to it, I had a sinking feeling in my chest, like a child who knew they were about to be caught in a lie. When I swung open the door, you were standing there by the bales of hay, holding my grandad's knife, and promising me in your cool, convincing voice that it wouldn't hurt too badly.

I didn't run, I didn't fight. Like the cow, I think the life had left me long before this moment. I quietly laid my naked body down in the hay. You dug the cold tip of the knife into my forehead, then with a sheepish smile, ripped it downwards. It made an incision straight down my neck, between my breasts, through my navel, to my pelvis. For a moment, you stopped to look at what you had done. Then you dug your hands into the gore, and began to turn me inside out. You told me you were going to find the piece of battery. Stubborn and tough like my grandad, though perhaps not as wise, you couldn't bury me until you had the satisfaction of knowing for certain what poison had sent our love to its premature death.

You dug and dug, blood staining your hands, your shirt, your eyes, but nothing unnatural was to be found. Fed up, you turned to leave the shed, when there was a quiet rustling from my open body. You turned and watched a little grey creature pull its feeble way out of my ribs and toss itself onto the hay. It was shaky and ugly and barely breathing.

Hearing its soft cry, I rose up, and with my shredded skin and my gaping torso and all the blood and tissue pouring out of me, I cradled the little thing for a moment. Then, weeping, I laid it down at your feet. With big eyes, I watched the dreamscape in gut-wrenching anticipation. I wanted so badly for you to pick the ugly thing up and hold it in your big arms, whisper love in its ear, coax life back into its weak frame. But I knew you, and I knew it wasn't the answer you were looking for when you cut me open, this little piece of life. I knew very well you might leave it there at your feet, cold and shivering, to die a crumpled soul in the hay, without even a manger to meet God in.

I woke before I got my answer.

If I timed this correctly, you've just gotten home from your Tuesday shift. You probably just tossed your coat by the door and opened up the fridge, when you saw the letter left on the table. I know this both a dramatic and a cowardly way to do this, but I can't seem to get the words out in person. Besides, I'm not quite sure what it is I want to say.

I should start by saying that I do love you, you know. I love your deep brown eyes and your third-floor bedroom and the way you come alive in the summer. I love the way my name rolls off your tongue in the early morning hours, and the way you stand with one foot cocked as you make your coffee. I love when you lose your patience and when you yell like a kid and when you apologize because you think it's the right thing to do.

But, and I can hear you protesting already, you don't really love me. You cannot truly love me because you have absolutely no idea who I am. I have absolutely no idea who I am. You know me only as a dancer who has meticulously learned her routine, spending six months memorizing just where to put her feet while you lead.

I hope you know I don't write this in anger. I think sadness, perhaps, more than anything, and frustration with myself, but not anger. It's just I've been coming to realize we are falling apart at the seams because I have such little of myself to bring to the table. And I see you look at me with all this hurt in your eyes and I feel you want to tear my skin open to see what's hiding underneath. I can see you clench your fist around the knife and think about ripping it right through me, just for the satisfaction of knowing our love was poisoned.

I don't know where to go from here, so I am just going to be honest. It's easier to do with a pen in my hand. There's a version of me I've never told you about, one I thought you'd never have to meet, but she's been on my mind lately, like the story of the cow.

I never told you that I dyed my hair brown a few months before we met. That it used to be blonde and shaggy and fall nearly to my waist. I never told you I used to hide behind it, a confused and lost teenager who wanted anything but to be seen.

I never told you about the loss, or those haunted days just after Christmas. I never told you about coming home in an itchy black dress, holding my throbbing heart in my shaky thirteen-year-old hands, wondering how on earth I was going to shove it back into place. I never told you about walking through the rooms of my home and wondering where the familiarity went, talking myself off the bathroom floor. I never told you about learning to deal with the type of loneliness that leaves you denouncing God, but still whispering to Him late at night in hopes He might talk back. I never told you that I swam my way out of the great blue waves twice before, and it didn't make me stronger—it left me thinking I wouldn't be able to muster the strength do it again.

I never told you about how after the grass grew back over the upturned dirt, I spent nearly a decade powering through, being an easy-going, self-cleaning oven, who broke down alone and picked up the pieces alone. I never told you about how I never yelled, never wept, never lost my temper the way a teenager should. I never told you about how when I craved company, I turned to people who never asked me to be more than their mirror, and when I craved affection, I turned to hands who never tried to touch anything more than my body. I never told you how in never being vulnerable, I felt safe, because I never had to worry about being ripped to the ground again. How this way of life ensured I'd never be alone, while also never reliant on anyone but myself. I never told you about how in my young, twisted way I used to think that was strength. That I could walk away from any place, or any person, and say look at me, fuckers, I'm still standing.

I never told you because it's over now. It's been years and years since those days with my braces and my shaggy blonde hair and self-hatred and grief. She's a completely different person than the one writing to you now, separated by more than seven years and a tube of shitty box dye. But it frightens me that despite all that growth, if you were to rip me open as I am now, all you would find in my body is a child who's been hiding away for years. It frightens me that if you took a knife to my hide, you wouldn't find any poison or rotting toxins, just a shaky, little grey piece of soul you wouldn't know how to help. It frightens me to know that if I laid that undernourished, feeble creature down at your feet, and you chose to walk away, I would struggle to survive.

I am choosing to leave you and our months together here, sealed up in an envelope on your counter. Because instead of finding the courage to hand you that feeble child, I must first find the courage to hand her back to myself. I must cradle her against my beating heart, show her I love her unconditionally, nurture her, give her all my time and grace and energy, until she is strong and grown and unapologetically alive. Only when this is done can I rip myself open, and devote myself to other love.

Imago Dei

As I float between who I am and who I am becoming,
sometimes I can't help but get so dizzy, so groundless,
that I have to stop midday just to
swim in my uncertainty.

Sitting with the world in my throat
I close my eyes and go back to that familiar scene,
the little bench in the garden of roses and rectitude
where I can find my breath in the quiet pulse of creation.

When they open, I acknowledge I am not alone.
By a tree in the garden stands the man.
My heart jumps as I think of everything he is.
The strong arm and the warm hand and the young grin,
the tender piece of flesh above the groin,
the bulging muscle of the thigh.

When he walks over to the bench
my cheeks flush with swirls of heat
and I feel like I did when I was a young girl,
sitting on the edge of the schoolyard,
wide eyes and butterflies
watching the boy with the freckles and gapped teeth.

I've been waiting for you, I say, as he sits down on my right.
He rests his head on my shoulder,
and I think of everything I would give up
just to hold him
in my heart
and in my home
and in between my teeth,
forever.

But then, more subtly, in walks the woman.
She isn't as abrasive about it,
glowing in my periphery, her body bathes in sinking
hues of violet and blue,
I call to her: mum, sister, friend,
come join us in the shade!

But tasting my insincerity she just stands, wise and patient at
the threshold.

Frightened, I try to cling to the man,
but the violet of the woman bleeds into my vision
and covers the edges of my throat;
I can't breathe.

When I'm choking, gasping for air,
I let myself see it.
The soft meeting of her lips, the dip of her collar bone,
the curving fat of her waist.
There's a magic that dances around her
and a fiery blaze behind her eyes
that takes the wind from my lungs
and shoots the pulse of new life through my veins.

She frightens me.
For I can love the man as an outsider, I can love every inch
of him for everything I am not,
but I know the woman too deeply.

I know her pleasure and I know her plight
I know her beauty in admiration
and know it in envy—

But despite these fears, I also know
when she sits on my other side
I feel miraculously myself,
a hand in Adam's and a hand in Eve's.
I am powerful and alive.

Before I can run back in cowardice
they lean in and kiss the tender flesh
of my neck—
while I stare, steadfast and unbreaking,
into the eyes of God

and ask him if he likes his reflection.

Biography

Áine Griffin is a junior at Endicott College, where she is studying English and Secondary Education. Griffin is from South Boston, Massachusetts, but a piece of her heart will always be with her family in Connemara, Ireland. When she is not writing, she loves painting, rowing, having long conversations with friends, and getting perpetually distracted. She has previously been published in the Endicott Review and has received the Derby medal for an English poem.